I PRAY Heaven to bestow the best
of Blessings on this House
and all that shall hereafter inhabit it.
May none but honest and
wise Men ever rule under this roof.

—John Adams,
letter to Abigail Adams,
November 2, 1800

Four score and seven years ago our fa[thers brought]
forth, upon this continent, a new na[tion, conceived]
in liberty, and dedicated to the prop[osition that]
"all men are created equal"

Now we are engaged in a great civ[il war, testing]
whether that nation, or any nation[so conceived]
and so dedicated, can long endure, [We are met]
on a great battle field of that war. [We have]
come to dedicate a portion of it, as a [final rest]
ing place for those who died here, tha[t the nation]
might live. This we may, in all propriety d[o. But, in a]
larger sense, we can not dedicate— w[e can not]
consecrate— we can not hallow, thi[s ground—]
The brave men, living and dead, w[ho struggled]
here, have hallowed it, far above ou[r poor power]
to add or detract. The world will litt[le note, nor long]
remember what we say here; while it [can never]
forget what they did here.

It is rather for us, the living, to [*we here*]

SMITHSONIAN
Book of
PRESIDENTIAL
QUOTATIONS

SMITHSONIAN BOOKS · WASHINGTON, DC

© 2024 by Smithsonian Institution

Published by Smithsonian Books
Director: Carolyn Gleason
Senior Editor: Jaime Schwender
Editor: Julie Huggins

Designed by Robert L. Wiser

This book may be purchased for educational, business, or sales promotional use. For information, please write:

Special Markets Department, Smithsonian Books, PO Box 37012, MRC 513, Washington, DC 20013

Library of Congress Cataloging-in-Publication Data available.

ISBN: 978-1-58834-772-5

Printed in the United States of America

28 27 26 25 24   1 2 3 4 5

Front cover: Eleanor Parke Custis silhouette of George Washington (ca. 1798), Smithsonian's National Portrait Gallery. Page 2: Draft of Abraham Lincoln's Gettysburg Address (November 1863), courtesy of the Library of Congress. Page 7: NBC microphone used by Franklin D. Roosevelt (ca. 1932–45), Smithsonian's National Museum of American History (photograph by Richard Strauss). Page 10: Gilbert Stewart portrait of George Washington (1796), Smithsonian's National Portrait Gallery. For permission to reproduce illustrations appearing in this book, please correspond directly with the owners of the works.

Contents

Introduction

HARRY TRUMAN once said that the "greatest part of the President's job is to make decisions—big ones and small ones, dozens of them almost every day." Even though these decisions can change the course of human events, the president's job is largely done out of sight. We don't watch the president work, and we only learn about the decisions when the president tells us about them. Even then, most people don't hear the president's words firsthand; instead, they encounter clips and soundbites chosen by someone else. In spite of this limited visibility, perhaps even because of it, the words presidents choose shape their administrations and our future. We would do well to listen.

Today the president can speak to the public instantaneously, if not incessantly, and because, as Lyndon Johnson once said, the presidency is the only office that belongs to everyone, the words of presidents can appear to matter more than those of others. That was not always the case. From George Washington's Farewell Address to Andrew Jackson's Bank Veto to Lincoln's Gettysburg Address, some presidential statements captured the nation's attention in earlier years, but not many. Throughout the nineteenth century, most presidential "speeches"—including annual messages and State of the Union addresses—were not speeches at all but written statements delivered to Congress on paper and made available to the public through the press. Even presidential candidates rarely

NBC used this microphone to capture Franklin D. Roosevelt's
radio broadcasts, known as fireside chats, throughout his presidency.

campaigned in person; inaugural addresses were the only speeches expected to be given in person before a public audience. With just a few exceptions, the most eloquent speakers and the most important words came from Congress.

The balance of federal oratorical power started to shift from the legislative to the executive branch around the turn of the twentieth century. Rather than addressing Congress directly, especially when trying to advance an administration's agenda, presidents began taking their policies directly to the people, engaging them as allies in persuading lawmakers. While many factors influenced the emergence of what has come to be called the rhetorical presidency, one factor stands out: the evolution of communication technology.

The earliest presidential addresses appeared, usually in their entirety, in newspapers (some of which were highly partisan mouthpieces for the president's party). Speeches were even printed on fabric, such as silk, to keep and display presidential words (including the longest inaugural address in history, William Henry Harrison's at 8,445 words). The invention of sound and film recording made it possible for many more people to hear and see the president. In 1889, Benjamin Harrison was the first president recorded, but, in those days, the speeches were heavily excerpted. Film's potential began to be realized with Theodore Roosevelt (who was filmed more than one hundred times) and Woodrow Wilson, both of whom embraced technology and travel, believing they could speak directly to the American people without having to go through

Congress first. Radio's growth in the 1930s enabled the words of Franklin Roosevelt, a gifted public speaker, to go directly into millions of homes. Now, in real time, the president could share *all* his words with the world, without Congress or editors intervening. Communication technology kept growing and presidents kept making it work for them. As FDR had excelled at radio, John F. Kennedy succeeded on television, Bill Clinton experimented with the internet, and Barack Obama and Donald Trump used social media to spread their words.

Through statements printed, recorded, televised, and tweeted, words from the nation's communicator-in-chief have shaped administrations, our lives, and history itself. From Theodore Roosevelt's excitement over his "bully pulpit" to Woodrow Wilson's calling himself the spokesperson of the nation to Ronald Reagan's commitment to communicate great things from "the heart of a great nation," presidents have been profoundly aware of the importance and power of what they have to say. This volume gives you a taste of their words, from George Washington to Joe Biden, and from a variety of sources, representing the full range of rhetorical eras. No single speech is printed in full, but all presidents are represented in part. Explore these samples, read some full texts, listen to the speeches being given now and in the future. Decide for yourself which presidential words matter, and see where they might take us all.

—*E. Claire Jerry, Curator, Political History*
Smithsonian's National Museum of American History

❧ *George Washington* ☙

BORN: February 22, 1732
DIED: December 14, 1799
TERM: 1789–1797

KNOWLEDGE is in every country the surest basis of public happiness.
—*first annual message, January 8, 1790*

THE welfare of our Country is the great object to which our cares and efforts ought to be directed. And I shall derive great satisfaction from a co-operation with you, in the pleasing though arduous task of ensuring to our fellow Citizens the blessings, which they have a right to expect, from a free, efficient and equal Government.
—*first annual message, January 8, 1790*

I HOPE ever to see America among the foremost nations in examples of justice and liberality.
—*letter to Roman Catholics in America, March 15, 1790*

THE unity of government which constitutes you one people is also now dear to you. It is justly so, for it is a main pillar in the edifice of your real independence, the support of your tranquility at home, your peace abroad; of your safety; of your prosperity; of that very liberty which you so highly prize.
—*Farewell Address, September 19, 1796*

THE basis of our political systems is the right of the people to make and to alter their constitutions of government. But the constitution which at any time exists till changed by an explicit and authentic act of the whole people is sacredly obligatory upon all. The very idea of the power and the right of the people to establish government presupposes the duty of every individual to obey the established government.

—Farewell Address, September 19, 1796

❧ *John Adams* ☙

BORN: October 30, 1735
DIED: July 4, 1826
TERM: 1797–1801

THE existence of such a government as ours for any length of time is a full proof of a general dissemination of knowledge and virtue throughout the whole body of the people. And what object or consideration more pleasing than this can be presented to the human mind? If national pride is ever justifiable or excusable it is when it springs, not from power or riches, grandeur or glory, but from conviction of national innocence, information, and benevolence.

—inaugural address, March 4, 1797

MAY this territory be the residence of virtue and happiness! In this city may that piety and virtue, that wisdom and magnanimity, that constancy and self-government, which adorned the great character whose name it bears be forever held in veneration!

—*on the move of the federal government to Washington, DC, in his fourth annual message, November 22, 1800*

⚜ *Thomas Jefferson* ⚜

BORN: April 13, 1743
DIED: July 4, 1826
TERM: 1801–1809

ALL too will bear in mind this sacred principle, that though the will of the majority is in all cases to prevail, that will to be rightful must be reasonable; that the minority possess their equal rights, which equal laws must protect, and to violate would be oppression.

—*first inaugural address, March 4, 1801*

BELIEVING with you that religion is a matter which lies solely between Man & his God, that he owes account to none other for his faith or his worship, that the legitimate powers of government reach actions only, & not opinions, I contemplate with sovereign reverence that act of the whole American people which declared that their legislature should "make no law respecting an establishment of religion, or pro-hibiting the free exercise thereof," thus building a wall of separation between Church & State.

—*letter to the Danbury Baptist Association in Danbury, Connecticut, January 1, 1802*

THE object of your mission is to explore the Missouri river, & such principal stream of it, as, by its course & communication with the waters of the Pacific ocean may offer the most direct & practicable water communication across this continent, for the purposes of commerce.

—*instructions to Meriwether Lewis, June 20, 1803*

❧ James Madison ❧

BORN: March 16, 1751
DIED: June 28, 1836
TERM: 1809–1817

I REPAIR to the post assigned me with no other discouragement than what springs from my own inadequacy to its high duties. If I do not sink under the weight of this deep conviction it is because I find some support in a consciousness of the purposes and a confidence in the principles which I bring with me into this arduous service.

—*first inaugural address, March 4, 1809*

NOTWITHSTANDING the security for future repose which the United States ought to find in their love of peace and their constant respect for the rights of other nations, the character of the times particularly inculcates the lesson that, whether to prevent or repel danger, we ought not to be unprepared for it.

—*seventh annual message, December 5, 1815*

IT remains for the guardians of the public welfare to persevere in that justice and good will toward other nations which invite a return of these sentiments toward the United States; to cherish institutions which guarantee their safety and their liberties, civil and religious; and to combine with a liberal system of foreign commerce an improvement of the national advantages and a protection and extension of the independent resources of our highly favored and happy country.

—seventh annual message, December 5, 1815

❧ James Monroe ❧

BORN: April 28, 1758
DIED: July 4, 1831
TERM: 1817–1825

LET us by all wise and constitutional measures promote intelligence among the people as the best means of preserving our liberties.

—first inaugural address, Tuesday, March 4, 1817

As a principle in which the rights and interests of the United States are involved, that the American continents, by the free and independent condition which they have assumed and maintain, are henceforth not to be considered as subjects for future colonization by any European powers.

*—seventh annual address, known as the
Monroe Doctrine, December 2, 1823*

❧ John Quincy Adams ☙

BORN: July 11, 1767
DIED: February 23, 1848
TERM: 1825–1829

STANDING at this point of time, looking back to that generation which has gone by and forward to that which is advancing, we may at once indulge in grateful exultation and in cheering hope. From the experience of the past we derive instructive lessons for the future. Of the two great political parties which have divided the opinions and feelings of our country, the candid and the just will now admit that both have contributed splendid talents, spotless integrity, ardent patriotism, and disinterested sacrifices to the formation and administration of this Government, and that both have required a liberal indulgence for a portion of human infirmity and error.

—*inaugural address, March 4, 1825*

OUR political creed is, without a dissenting voice that can be heard, that the will of the people is the source and the happiness of the people the end of all legitimate government upon earth; that the best security for the beneficence and the best guaranty against the abuse of power consists in the freedom, the purity, and the frequency of popular elections.

—*inaugural address, March 4, 1825*

❧ *Andrew Jackson* ❧

BORN: March 15, 1767
DIED June 8, 1845
TERM: 1829–1837

As long as our government is administered for the good of the people, and is regulated by their will; as long as it secures to us the rights of person and of property, liberty of conscience, and of the press, it will be worth defending.

—*first inaugural address, March 4, 1829*

THE wisdom of man never yet contrived a system of taxation that would operate with perfect equality.

—*proclamation regarding the nullification laws of South Carolina, December 10, 1832*

Jackson issued this proclamation in response to an ordinance issued by a South Carolina convention declaring that the tariff acts of 1828 and 1832 went against the Constitution and therefore were void. South Carolina citizens felt that the acts favored the interests of Northern-based manufacturing at the expense of Southern farmers. Congress then issued the Force Act of 1833, authorizing President Jackson to enforce compliance through military action.

BUT you must remember, my fellow-citizens, that eternal vigilance by the people is the price of liberty, and that you must pay the price if you wish to secure the blessing.

—*farewell address, March 4, 1837*

❧ *Martin Van Buren* ❧

BORN: December 5, 1782
DIED: July 24, 1862
TERM: 1837–1841

ALL the lessons of history and experience must be lost
upon us if we are content to trust alone to the peculiar
advantages we happen to possess.

—inaugural address, March 4, 1837

IT was reserved for the American Union to test the
advantages of a government entirely dependent on the
continual exercise of the popular will, and our experience has shown that it is as beneficent in practice as it
is just in theory. Each successive change made in our
local institutions has contributed to extend the right
of suffrage, has increased the direct influence of the
mass of the community, given greater freedom to individual exertion, and restricted more and more the
powers of Government; yet the intelligence, prudence,
and patriotism of the people have kept pace with this
augmented responsibility. In no country has education
been so widely diffused. Domestic peace has nowhere
so largely reigned. The close bonds of social inter-
course have in no instance prevailed with such har-
mony over a space so vast.

—second annual message, December 3, 1838

❧ William Henry Harrison ❧

BORN: February 9, 1773
DIED: April 4, 1841
TERM: 1841

IF parties in a republic are necessary to secure a degree of vigilance sufficient to keep the public functionaries within the bounds of law and duty, at that point their usefulness ends. Beyond that they become destructive of public virtue, the parent of a spirit antagonist to that of liberty, and eventually its inevitable conqueror.
—*inaugural address, March 4, 1841*

THE people of the District of Columbia are not the subjects of the people of the States, but free American citizens.

—*inaugural address, March 4, 1841*

❧ John Tyler ❧

BORN: March 29, 1790
DIED: January 18, 1862
TERM: 1841–1845

FOR the first time in our history the person elected to the Vice-Presidency of the United States, by the happening of a contingency provided for in the Constitution, has had devolved upon him the Presidential office.
—*address upon assuming the presidency after the death of William Henry Harrison, April 9, 1841*

WE hold out to the people of other countries an invitation to come and settle among us as members of our rapidly growing family, and for the blessings which we offer them we require of them to look upon our country as their country and to unite with us in the great task of preserving our institutions and thereby perpetuating our liberties.

—special session message to Congress regarding general affairs of the country, June 1, 1841

❧ James K. Polk ❧

BORN: November 2, 1795
DIED: June 15, 1849
TERM: 1845–1849

As the wisdom, strength, and beneficence of our free institutions are unfolded, every day adds fresh motives to contentment and fresh incentives to patriotism.

—second annual message, December 8, 1846

PEACE, plenty, and contentment reign throughout our borders, and our beloved country presents a sublime moral spectacle to the world.

—fourth annual message, December 5, 1848

THAT the majority should govern is a general principle controverted by none, but they must govern according to the Constitution, and not according to an undefined and unrestrained discretion, whereby they may oppress the minority.

—fourth annual message, December 5, 1848

❧ Zachary Taylor ❧

BORN: November 24, 1784
DIED: July 9, 1850
TERM: 1849–1850

ATTACHMENT to the Union of the States should be habitually fostered in every American heart.

—annual message, December 4, 1849

CONNECTED, as the Union is, with the remembrance of past happiness, the sense of present blessings, and the hope of future peace and prosperity, every dictate of wisdom, every feeling of duty, and every emotion of patriotism tend to inspire fidelity and devotion to it and admonish us cautiously to avoid any unnecessary controversy which can either endanger it or impair its strength, the chief element of which is to be found in the regard and affection of the people for each other.

—message regarding newly acquired
territories, January 23, 1850

In 1849, residents of California sought statehood and to be admitted as a non-slaveholding state, which sparked a debate in Congress about slavery for territories and new states. Through his message, Taylor expressed that the question of slavery should be left to the citizens of the state and not dictated by Congress. In September 1850, California was admitted as the 31st state, and was allowed to outlaw slavery within the state.

❧ Millard Fillmore ☙

BORN: January 7, 1800
DIED: March 8, 1874
TERM: 1850–1853

OUR liberties, religious and civil, have been maintained, the fountains of knowledge have all been kept open, and means of happiness widely spread and generally enjoyed, greater than have fallen to the lot of any other nation. And while deeply penetrated with gratitude for the past, let us hope that His all-wise providence will so guide our counsels as that they shall result in giving satisfaction to our constituents, securing the peace of the country, and adding new strength to the united Government under which we live.

—*first annual message, December 2, 1850*

ENJOYING, as we do, the blessings of a free Government, there is no man who has an American heart that would not rejoice to see these blessings extended to all other nations.

—third annual message, December 6, 1852

❧ *Franklin Pierce* ☙

BORN: November 23, 1804
DIED: October 8, 1869
TERM: 1853–1857

THE circumstances under which I have been called for a limited period to preside over the destinies of the Republic fill me with a profound sense of responsibility, but with nothing like shrinking apprehension.

—inaugural address, March 4, 1853

WHILE the different branches of the Government are to a certain extent independent of each other, the duties of all alike have direct reference to the source of power. Fortunately, under this system no man is so high and none so humble in the scale of public station as to escape from the scrutiny or to be exempt from the responsibility which all official functions imply.

—first annual message, December 5, 1853

❧ James Buchanan ❧

BORN: April 23, 1791
DIED: June 1, 1868
TERM: 1857–1861

CONGRESS has also prescribed that when the Territory of Kansas shall be admitted as a State it "shall be received into the Union with or without slavery, as their constitution may prescribe at the time of their admission." A difference of opinion has arisen in regard to the point of time when the people of a Territory shall decide this question for themselves.

This is, happily, a matter of but little practical importance.

—*inaugural address, March 4, 1857*

Multiple constitutions were written for the Kansas Territory both in support of and in opposition to slavery during a time of constant upheaval and violent confrontations known as Bleeding Kansas (1854–1859). After what was seen as a fraudulent election, the state constitution submitted to Congress included pro-slavery sentiments, but was rejected. The question of whether a territory had to settle the issue of slavery before becoming a state was hotly debated. Kansas was admitted to the Union as a non-slaveholding state in 1861, after representatives from Southern states had seceded.

I FEEL that my duty has been faithfully, though it may be imperfectly, performed, and, whatever the result may be, I shall carry to my grave the consciousness that I at least meant well for my country.

—*speech to Congress, January 8, 1861*

❧ *Abraham Lincoln* ❧

BORN: February 12, 1809
DIED: April 15, 1865
TERM: 1861–1865

OUR popular Government has often been called an experiment. Two points in it our people have already settled—the successful establishing and the successful administering of it. One still remains—its successful maintenance against a formidable internal attempt to overthrow it. It is now for them to demonstrate to the world that those who can fairly carry an election can also suppress a rebellion; that ballots are the rightful and peaceful successors of bullets, and that when ballots have fairly and constitutionally decided there can be no successful appeal back to bullets; that there can be no successful appeal except to ballots themselves at succeeding elections. Such will be a great lesson of peace, teaching men that what they can not take by an election neither can they take it by a war; teaching all the folly of being the beginners of a war.

—*July 4th message to Congress, July 4, 1861*

ALL persons held as slaves within any State or designated part of a State, the people whereof shall then be in rebellion against the United States, shall be then, thenceforward, and forever free; and the Executive Government of the United States, including the military and naval authority thereof, will recognize and maintain the freedom of such persons, and will do no

act or acts to repress such persons, or any of them, in any efforts they may make for their actual freedom.
—*Emancipation Proclamation, January 1, 1863*

You say you will not fight to free negroes. Some of them seem willing to fight for you; but, no matter. Fight you, then, exclusively to save the Union. I issued the proclamation on purpose to aid you in saving the Union.
—*public letter read by James Conkling at a rally in Springfield, Illinois, August 26, 1863*

THE brave men, living and dead, who struggled here, have consecrated it, far above our poor power to add or detract. The world will little note, nor long remember what we say here, but it can never forget what they did here.
—*Gettysburg Address, November 19, 1863*

I AM naturally anti-slavery. If slavery is not wrong, nothing is wrong.
—*publicly distributed letter to Albert G. Hodges, editor of the Frankfort, Kentucky,* Commonwealth, *April 4, 1864*

WITH malice toward none, with charity for all, with firmness in the fight as God gives us to see the right, let us strive on to finish the work we are in, to bind up the nation's wounds, to care for him who shall have borne the battle and for his widow and his orphan, to do all which may achieve and cherish a just and lasting peace among ourselves and with all nations.
—*second inaugural address, March 4, 1865*

❧ Andrew Johnson ❧

BORN: December 29, 1808
DIED: July 31, 1875
TERM: 1865–1869

I FEEL incompetent to perform duties so important and responsible as those which have been so unexpectedly thrown upon me.

*—first address to his cabinet after
Lincoln's assassination, April 15, 1865*

OUR Government springs from and was made for the people—not the people for the Government. To them it owes allegiance; from them it must derive its courage, strength, and wisdom.

—first annual message, December 4, 1865

❧ Ulysses S. Grant ❧

BORN: April 27, 1822
DIED: July 23, 1885
TERM: 1869–1877

THE country having just emerged from a great rebellion, many questions will come before it for settlement in the next four years which preceding Administrations have never had to deal with. In meeting these, it is desirable that they should be approached calmly, without prejudice, hate, or sectional pride, remembering that the greatest good to the greatest number is the object to be attained.

—first inaugural address, March 4, 1869

I WOULD protect the law-abiding citizen, whether of native or foreign birth, wherever his rights are jeopardized or the flag of our country floats.

—first inaugural address, March 4, 1869

THE framers of our Constitution firmly believed that a republican government could not endure without intelligence and education generally diffused among the people.

—special message to the Senate and
House of Representatives, March 30, 1870

TREAT the negro as a citizen and a voter, as he is and must remain, and soon parties will be divided, not on the color line, but on principle.

—sixth annual message, December 7, 1874

❧ *Rutherford B. Hayes* ❧

BORN: October 4, 1822
DIED: January 17, 1893
TERM: 1877–1881

THE President of the United States of necessity owes his election to office to the suffrage and zealous labors of a political party, the members of which cherish with ardor and regard as of essential importance the principles of their party organization; but he should strive to be always mindful of the fact that he serves his party best who serves the country best.

—*inaugural address, March 5, 1977*

THE people of this country are unwilling to see the supremacy of the Constitution replaced by the omnipotence of any one department of the Government.

—*veto of the Army appropriations bill, April 29, 1879*

In 1879 the House of Representatives passed an Army appropriations bill that included language forbidding the use of federal troops at polls to keep the peace. Many saw this as an attempt to undermine the safety of Black voters, who often faced violence at the polls after being given the right to vote. Hayes vetoed the bill.

James Garfield

BORN: November 19, 1831
DIED: September 19, 1881
TERM: 1881

THERE can be no permanent disfranchised peasantry in the United States. Freedom can never yield its fullness of blessings so long as the law or its administration places the smallest obstacle in the pathway of any virtuous citizen.

—*inaugural address, March 4, 1881*

It is the high privilege and sacred duty of those now living to educate their successors and fit them, by intelligence and virtue, for the inheritance which awaits them. In this beneficent work, sections and races should be forgotten and partisanship should be unknown. Let our people find a new meaning in the divine oracle which declares that "a little child shall lead them," for our own little children will soon control the destinies of the Republic.

—inaugural address, March 4, 1881

❧ Chester A. Arthur ☙

BORN: October 5, 1829
DIED: November 18, 1886
TERM: 1881–1885

MEN may die, but the fabrics of our free institutions remain unshaken.

—address upon assuming the presidency after the assassination of James Garfield, September 22, 1881

As is natural with contiguous states having like institutions and like aims of advancement and development, the friendship of the United States and Mexico has been constantly maintained.

—first annual message, December 6, 1881

❧ Grover Cleveland ❧

BORN: March 18, 1837
DIED: June 24, 1908
FIRST TERM: 1885–1889
SECOND TERM: 1893–1897

WE will not forget that liberty has here made her home; nor shall her chosen altar be neglected. Willing votaries will constantly keep alive its fires, and these shall gleam upon the shores of our sister republic in the East. Reflected thence and joined with answering rays, a stream of light shall pierce the darkness of ignorance and man's oppression, until liberty enlightens the world.

—*dedication speech for the*
Statue of Liberty, October 28, 1886

A CAUSE worth fighting for is worth fighting for to the end.
—*letter to the* New York Herald, *published June 16, 1896*

Cleveland was pushing against the usage of silver to back paper currency, a popular platform of William Jennings Bryan, who was running for the office of president. Though Cleveland and Bryan belonged to the same party, Cleveland was opposed to Bryan's populist silver platform.

IT is said, however, that the quality of recent immigration is undesirable. The time is quite within recent memory when the same thing was said of immigrants who, with their descendants, are now numbered among our best citizens.

—*veto message regarding immigration legislation, March 2, 1897*

Cleveland vetoed an act that would have banned illiterate immigrants from entering the United States.

❧ *Benjamin Harrison* ☙

BORN: August 20, 1833
DIED: March 13, 1901
TERM: 1889–1893

I DO not mistrust the future.

—*inaugural address, March 4, 1889*

No other people have a government more worthy of their respect and love or a land so magnificent in extent, so pleasant to look upon, and so full of generous suggestion to enterprise and labor. God has placed upon our head a diadem and has laid at our feet power and wealth beyond definition or calculation. But we must not forget that we take these gifts upon the condition that justice and mercy shall hold the reins of power and that the upward avenues of hope shall be free to all the people.

—*inaugural address, March 4, 1889*

WHEN the harvests from the fields, the cattle from the hills, and the ores of the earth shall have been weighed, counted, and valued, we will turn from them all to crown with the highest honor the State that has most promoted education, virtue, justice, and patriotism among its people.

—*inaugural address, March 4, 1889*

❧ William McKinley ☙

BORN: January 29, 1843
DIED: September 14, 1901
TERM: 1897–1901

FINALLY, it should be the earnest wish and paramount aim of the military administration to win the confidence, respect, and affection of the inhabitants of the Philippines by assuring them in every possible way that full measure of individual rights and liberties which is the heritage of free peoples, and by proving to them that the mission of the United States is one of BENEVOLENT ASSIMILATION.

—*Benevolent Assimilation Proclamation,
December 21, 1898*

"Benevolent assimilation" refers to the United States's policy on the Philippines following the Spanish–American War of 1898. McKinley declared that control and government of the Philippines had been ceded to the United States from Spain and that the US military should establish and maintain control of the territory, despite the Filipino citizens fighting for freedom from both Spain and the United States.

GENTLEMEN, let us ever remember that our interest is in concord, not conflict, and that our real eminence rests in the victories of peace, not those of war.
—*last public utterance before his assassination, to an audience in Buffalo, New York, September 5, 1901*

❧ Theodore Roosevelt ❧

BORN: October 27, 1858
DIED: January 6, 1919
TERM: 1901–1909

THE forest reserves should be set apart forever for the use and benefit of our people as a whole and not sacrificed to the shortsighted greed of a few.
—*first annual message, December 3, 1901*

I DON'T pity any man who does hard work worth doing. I admire him. I pity the creature who does not work, at whichever end of the social scale he may regard himself as being. The law of worthy work well done is the law of successful American life.
—*remarks to the Brotherhood of Locomotive Firemen in Chattanooga, Tennessee, September 8, 1902*

THE welfare of each of us is dependent fundamentally upon the welfare of all of us, and therefore in public life that man is the best representative of each of us who seeks to do good to each by doing good to all.

—*speech to farmers at the New York State Agricultural Association, Syracuse, New York, September 7, 1903*

MUCH has been given us, and much will rightfully be expected from us. We have duties to others and duties to ourselves; and we can shirk neither.

—*inaugural address, March 4, 1905*

THIS country has nothing to fear from the crooked man who fails. We put him in jail. It is the crooked man who succeeds who is a threat to this country.

—*address in Memphis, Tennessee, October 25, 1905*

WE of an older generation can get along with what we have, though with growing hardship; but in your full manhood and womanhood you will want what nature once bountifully supplied and man so thoughtlessly destroyed; and because of this want you will reproach us, not for what we have used, but for what we have wasted. . . . So any nation which in its youth lives only for the day, reaps without sowing, and consumes without husbanding, must expect the penalty of the prodigal whose labor could with difficulty find him the bare means of life.

—*Arbor Day letter to America's children, April 15, 1907*

❧ William Howard Taft ❧

BORN: September 15, 1857
DIED: March 8, 1930
TERM: 1909–1913

ANYONE who has taken the oath I have just taken must feel a heavy weight of responsibility.
—inaugural address, March 4, 1909

I AM in favor of helping the prosperity of all countries because, when we are all prosperous, the trade of each becomes more valuable to the other.
—address at a banquet at the Hotel Fairmont,
San Francisco, California, October 5, 1909

❧ Woodrow Wilson ❧

BORN: December 28, 1856
DIED: February 3, 1924
TERM: 1913–1921

IF you think too much about being re-elected, it is very difficult to be worth re-electing.
—rededication of Congress Hall,
Philadelphia, Pennsylvania, October 25, 1913

I WOULD rather belong to a poor nation that was free than to a rich nation that had ceased to be in love with liberty. But we shall not be poor if we love liberty, because the nation that loves liberty truly sets every man free to do his best and be his best, and that means the release of all the splendid energies of a great people who think for themselves.

—address on Latin American policy before the Southern Commercial Congress in Mobile, Alabama, October 27, 1913

THERE is one choice we cannot make, we are incapable of making: we will not choose the path of submission and suffer the most sacred rights of our Nation and our people to be ignored or violated. The wrongs against which we now array ourselves are no common wrongs; they cut to the very roots of human life.

—address to a joint session of Congress requesting a declaration of war against Germany, April 2, 1917

THE world must be made safe for democracy. Its peace must be planted upon the tested foundations of political liberty.

—address to a joint session of Congress requesting a declaration of war against Germany, April 2, 1917

THE present and all that it holds belongs to the nations and the peoples who preserve their self-control and the orderly processes of their governments; the future to those who prove themselves the true friends of mankind. To conquer with arms is to make only a temporary conquest; to conquer the world by earning its esteem is to make permanent conquest.

—address to a joint session of Congress concerning the terms of armistice signed by Germany, November 11, 1918

❧ Warren G. Harding ❧

BORN: November 2, 1865
DIED: August 2, 1923
TERM: 1921–1923

A REGRET for the mistakes of yesterday must not,
however, blind us to the tasks of today.
— *inaugural address, March 4, 1921*

Harding denounced those in the United States who profited off
of World War I. He then noted that regrets about profiteering
in the face of countless deaths during war should not blind the
populace to the problems that followed the war.

WITH the nation-wide induction of womanhood into
our political life, we may count upon her intuitions,
her refinements, her intelligence, and her influence to
exalt the social order. We count upon her exercise of
the full privileges and the performance of the duties of
citizenship to speed the attainment of the highest state.
— *inaugural address, March 4, 1921*

EVERY funeral, every memorial, every tribute is for the
living—an offering in compensation of sorrow. When
the light of life goes out there is a new radiance in
eternity, and somehow the glow of it relieves the darkness which is left behind.
— *speech upon arrival of World War I
dead for burial, May 23, 1921*

I BELIEVE the gratitude of action vastly surpasses that of words.

—*Memorial Day address at Arlington*
National Cemetery, May 30, 1923

I WISH we might have less condemnation of error and more commendation of right. We ought to have much less of bitter criticism of errors and more of approval and appreciation for things well done.

—*Memorial Day address at Arlington*
National Cemetery, May 30, 1923

❧ *Calvin Coolidge* ☙

BORN: July 4, 1872
DIED: January 5, 1933
TERM: 1923–1929

THE world has had enough of the curse of hatred and selfishness, of destruction and war. It has had enough of the wrongful use of material power. For the healing of the nations there must be good will and charity, confidence and peace.

—*first annual message, December 6, 1923*

FAITH in the American people means a faith in their ability to form sound judgments, when once the facts have been presented to them clearly and without prejudice.

—*address to the annual luncheon of the*
Associated Press in New York City, April 22, 1924

THE progress of the world rests on courage, honor and faith. If America wishes to maintain its prosperity, it must maintain its ideals.

*—address to the annual luncheon of the
Associated Press in New York City, April 22, 1924*

I FAVOR the policy of economy, not because I wish to save money, but because I wish to save people. The men and women of this country who toil are the ones who bear the cost of the Government. Every dollar that we carelessly waste means that their life will be so much the more meager. Every dollar that we prudently save means that their life will be so much the more abundant. Economy is idealism in its most practical form.

—inaugural address, March 4, 1925

PERHAPS one of the most important accomplishments of my administration has been the minding of my own business.

—press conference, March 1, 1929

⚜ *Herbert Hoover* ⚜

BORN: August 10, 1874
DIED: October 20, 1964
TERM: 1929–1933

THE United States fully accepts the profound truth that our own progress, prosperity, and peace are interlocked with the progress, prosperity, and peace of all humanity.

—inaugural address, March 4, 1929

BUT the government is that of the whole people; the party is the instrument through which policies are determined and men chosen to bring them into being. The animosities of elections should have no place in our Government, for government must concern itself alone with the common weal.

—inaugural address, March 4, 1929

WE must not be misled by the claim that the source of all wisdom is in the Government. We know that the source of wisdom is in the people; that the people can win anew the victory.

—Memorial Day address at Valley
Forge, Pennsylvania, May 30, 1931

❧ Franklin D. Roosevelt ❧

BORN: January 30, 1882
DIED: April 12, 1945
TERM: 1933–1945

THE only thing we have to fear is fear itself.

—first inaugural address, March 4, 1933

In his first inaugural address, Roosevelt reaffirmed to the American people that his administration was up to the task of overcoming the Great Depression. He told citizens that they should only be afraid of fear that can lead to inaction and an inability to progress.

MEN and nature must work hand in hand. The throwing out of balance of the resources of nature throws out of balance also the lives of men.

—message to Congress on the use of national resources, January 24, 1935

THE test of our progress is not whether we add more to the abundance of those who have much; it is whether we provide enough for those who have too little.

—second inaugural address, January 20, 1937

I NEVER forget that I live in a house owned by all the American people and that I have been given their trust.

—fireside chat, April 14, 1938

WE must scrupulously guard the civil rights and civil liberties of all our citizens, whatever their background. We must remember that any oppression, any injustice, any hatred, is a wedge designed to attack our civilization.

—greeting to the American Committee for Protection of Foreign Born, January 9, 1940

WE must be the great arsenal of Democracy.

—fireside chat, December 29, 1940

YESTERDAY, December 7, 1941—a date which will live in infamy—the United States of America was suddenly and deliberately attacked by naval and air forces of the Empire of Japan.

—address to Congress after the attack on Pearl Harbor, December 8, 1941

In the days and in the years that are to come we shall work for a just and honorable peace, a durable peace, as today we work and fight for total victory in war. We can and we will achieve such a peace.

—*fourth inaugural address, January 20, 1945*

❧ *Harry S. Truman* ☙

BORN: May 8, 1884
DIED: December 26, 1972
TERM: 1945–1953

We think of those whom death in this war has hurt, taking from them fathers, husbands, sons, brothers, and sisters whom they loved. No victory can bring back the faces they longed to see. Only the knowledge that the victory, which these sacrifices have made possible, will be wisely used, can give them any comfort. It is our responsibility—ours, the living—to see to it that this victory shall be a monument worthy of the dead who died to win it.

—*announcement of the surrender of Japan, September 1, 1945*

Our forefathers came to our rugged shores in search of religious tolerance, political freedom and economic opportunity. For those fundamental rights, they risked their lives. We well know today that such rights can be preserved only by constant vigilance, the eternal price of liberty!

—*first speech to Congress, April 16, 1946*

No government is perfect. One of the chief virtues of a democracy, however, is that its defects are always visible and under democratic processes can be pointed out and corrected.

—*special message to Congress on Greece and Turkey, known as the Truman Doctrine, March 12, 1947*

WHETHER discrimination is based on race, or creed, or color, or land of origin, it is utterly contrary to American ideals of democracy.

—*third State of the Union address, January 7, 1948*

IF history has taught us anything, it is that aggression anywhere in the world is a threat to the peace everywhere in the world.

—*report to the American people on Korea, April 11, 1952*

In this radio address, Truman defended the American military presence in Korea, suggesting that it was preventing a third world war.

THE greatest part of the President's job is to make decisions—big ones and small ones, dozens of them almost every day. The papers may circulate around the Government for a while but they finally reach this desk. And then, there's no place else for them to go. The President—whoever he is—has to decide. He can't pass the buck to anybody. No one else can do the deciding for him. That's his job.

—*farewell address, January 15, 1953*

❧ *Dwight D. Eisenhower* ❧

BORN: October 14, 1890
DIED: March 28, 1969
TERM: 1953–1961

FOR history does not long entrust the care of freedom to the weak or the timid.
>—*first inaugural address, January 20, 1953*

THE free world knows, out of the bitter wisdom of experience, that vigilance and sacrifice are the price of liberty.
>—*speech to the American Society of Newspaper Editors, "The Chance for Peace," April 16, 1953*

DON'T join the book burners. Don't think you are going to conceal faults by concealing evidence that they ever existed. Don't be afraid to go in your library and read every book, as long as that document does not offend our own ideas of decency. That should be the only censorship.
>—*remarks at the Dartmouth College commencement, Hanover, New Hampshire, June 14, 1953*

SOME politician some years ago said that bad officials are elected by good voters who do not vote.
>—*remarks at the breakfast meeting of Republican state chairmen in Denver, Colorado, September 10, 1955*

THE world moves, and ideas that were good once are not always good.
>—*news conference, August 31, 1956*

✤ John F. Kennedy ✤

BORN: May 29, 1917
DIED: November 22, 1963
TERM: 1961–1963

LET us never negotiate out of fear. But let us never fear to negotiate.
—*inaugural address, January 20, 1961*

MY fellow citizens of the world: ask not what America will do for you, but what together we can do for the freedom of man.
—*inaugural address, January 20, 1961*

WE dare not forget today that we are the heirs of that first revolution. Let the word go forth from this time and place, to friend and foe alike, that the torch has been passed to a new generation of Americans—born in this century, tempered by war, disciplined by a hard and bitter peace, proud of our ancient heritage—and unwilling to witness or permit the slow undoing of those human rights to which this nation has always been committed, and to which we are committed today at home and around the world.
—*inaugural address, January 20, 1961*

WE choose to go to the moon. We choose to go to the moon in this decade and do the other things, not because they are easy, but because they are hard, because that goal will serve to organize and measure the best of our energies and skills, because that challenge is one that we are willing to accept, one we are unwilling to postpone, and one which we intend to win, and the others, too.

—address at Rice University on the nation's space effort, September 12, 1962

A MAN may die, nations may rise and fall, but an idea lives on.

—remarks recorded for the opening of a USIA transmitter, Greenville, North Carolina, February 8, 1963

FREEDOM is indivisible, and when one man is enslaved, all are not free. When all are free, then we can look forward to that day when this city will be joined as one and this country and this great Continent of Europe in a peaceful and hopeful globe. When that day finally comes, as it will, the people of West Berlin can take sober satisfaction in the fact that they were in the front lines for almost two decades.

—"Ich bin ein Berliner" address at Rathaus Schöneberg, West Berlin, Germany, June 26, 1963

MY fellow Americans, let us take that first step. Let us . . . step back from the shadow of war and seek out the way of peace. And if that journey is a thousand miles, or even more, let history record that we, in this land, at this time, took the first step.

—radio and television address to the American people on the Nuclear Test Ban Treaty, July 26, 1963

❧ *Lyndon B. Johnson* ❧

BORN: August 27, 1908
DIED: January 22, 1973
TERM: 1963–1969

THE time has come for Americans of all races and creeds and political beliefs to understand and to respect one another. So let us put an end to the teaching and the preaching of hate and evil and violence. Let us turn away from the fanatics of the far left and the far right, from the apostles of bitterness and bigotry, from those defiant of law, and those who pour venom into our Nation's bloodstream.

—address to a joint session of Congress, November 27, 1963

THIS administration today, here and now, declares unconditional war on poverty in America. I urge this Congress and all Americans to join with me in that effort.

—first State of the Union address, January 8, 1964

LET me make one principle of this administration abundantly clear: All of these increased opportunities—in employment, in education, in housing, and in every field—must be open to Americans of every color. As far as the writ of Federal law will run, we must abolish not some, but all racial discrimination. For this is not merely an economic issue, or a social, political, or international issue. It is a moral issue.

—first State of the Union address, January 8, 1964

THE war on poverty is not a struggle simply to support people, to make them dependent on the generosity of others. It is a struggle to give people a chance. It is an effort to allow them to develop and use their capacities, as we have been allowed to develop and use ours, so that they can share, as others share, in the promise of this nation. We do this, first of all, because it is right that we should.

—special message to Congress on nationwide war on the sources of poverty, March 16, 1964

WE are all fellow passengers on a dot of earth. And each of us, in the span of time, has really only a moment among our companions. How incredible it is that in this fragile existence, we should hate and destroy one another. There are possibilities enough for all who will abandon mastery over others to pursue mastery over nature. There is world enough for all to seek their happiness in their own way.

—inaugural address, January 20, 1965

WE cannot have government for all the people until we first make certain it is government of and by all the people.

—special message to Congress on the right to vote, March 15, 1965

THERE is no room for injustice anywhere in the American mansion. But there is always room for understanding toward those who see the old ways crumbling. And to them, today, I simply say this: It must come. It is right that it should come. And when it has, you will find that a burden has been lifted from your shoulders, too.

—*remarks on the signing of the*
Voting Rights Act, August 6, 1965

❧ Richard M. Nixon ❧

BORN: January 9, 1913
DIED: April 22, 1994
TERM: 1969–1974

THE American dream does not come to those who fall asleep.

—*first inaugural address, January 20, 1969*

WHAT is even more important is not to think in terms of whether a woman could or should be President, but I think we should all say that by reason of the role women have played in politics in America a woman can and should be able to do any political job that a man could do.

—*remarks commemorating the 50th anniversary of the*
League of Women Voters of the United States, April 17, 1969

HELLO, Neil and Buzz. I'm talking to you by telephone from the Oval Room at the White House. And this certainly has to be the most historic telephone call ever made. For every American this has to be the proudest day of our lives. And for people all over the world I am sure they, too, join with Americans in recognizing what a feat this is. Because of what you have done, the heavens have become a part of man's world. As you talk to us from the Sea of Tranquility, it inspires us to redouble our efforts to bring peace and tranquility to Earth. For one priceless moment, in the whole history of man, all the people on this Earth are truly one.

—*telephone message from the Oval Office to Neil Armstrong and Buzz Aldrin on the Moon, July 20, 1969*

I WANT to say this to the television audience. I made my mistakes, but in all of my years of public life, I have never profited, never profited from public service. I have earned every cent. And in all of my years of public life, I have never obstructed justice. And I think, too, that I can say that in my years of public life, that I welcome this kind of examination because people have got to know whether or not their President is a crook. Well, I'm not a crook. I've earned everything I've got.

—*press conference at the convention of the Associated Press Managing Editors Association, November 17, 1973*

This quotation is the response to a question about Nixon's taxes and other personal finances. The Watergate scandal, which was being investigated at the time, led to increased scrutiny for all aspects of the president's life.

❧ Gerald R. Ford ❧

BORN: July 14, 1913
DIED: December 26, 2006
TERM: 1974–1977

THERE is no way we can go forward except together and no way anybody can win except by serving the people's urgent needs. We cannot stand still or slip backwards. We must go forward now together.
—*remarks upon taking the presidential oath after the resignation of Richard Nixon, August 9, 1974*

LIBERTY is for all men and women as a matter of equal and unalienable right. The establishment of justice and peace abroad will in large measure depend upon the peace and justice we create here in our own country, for we still show the way.
—*bicentennial remarks at Independence Hall, Philadelphia, Pennsylvania, July 4, 1976*

❧ James "Jimmy" Carter ❧

BORN: October 1, 1924
TERM: 1977–1981

LET us learn together and laugh together and work together and pray together, confident that in the end we will triumph together in the right.
—*inaugural address, January 20, 1977*

HUMAN rights is the soul of our foreign policy, because human rights is the very soul of our sense of nationhood.

—remarks commemorating the thirtieth anniversary of the Universal Declaration of Human Rights, December 6, 1978

HISTORY teaches, perhaps, very few clear lessons. But surely one such lesson learned by the world at great cost is that aggression, unopposed, becomes a contagious disease.

—speech on the December 24, 1979, Soviet invasion of Afghanistan, January 4, 1980

THERE are real and growing dangers to our simple and our most precious possessions: the air we breathe, the water we drink, and the land which sustains us. The rapid depletion of irreplaceable minerals, the erosion of topsoil, the destruction of beauty, the blight of pollution, the demands of increasing billions of people, all combine to create problems which are easy to observe and predict, but difficult to resolve.

—farewell address, January 14, 1981

DEMOCRACY is always an unfinished creation. Each generation must renew its foundations. Each generation must rediscover the meaning of this hallowed vision in the light of its own modern challenges.

—farewell address, January 14, 1981

❧ *Ronald Reagan* ❧

BORN: February 6, 1911
DIED: June 5, 2004
TERM: 1981–1989

WE have every right to dream heroic dreams. Those who say that we're in a time when there are not heroes, they just don't know where to look.
—first inaugural address, January 20, 1981

PRESERVATION of our environment is not a liberal or conservative challenge, it's common sense.
—third State of the Union address, January 25, 1984

THERE are no constraints on the human mind, no walls around the human spirit, no barriers to our progress except those we ourselves erect.
—fourth State of the Union address, February 6, 1985

WE cannot play innocents abroad in a world that's not innocent; nor can we be passive when freedom is under siege.
—fourth State of the Union address, February 6, 1985

THE future doesn't belong to the fainthearted; it belongs to the brave. The *Challenger* crew was pulling us into the future, and we'll continue to follow them.
—address to the nation on the explosion of the Space Shuttle Challenger, *January 28, 1986*

MR. Gorbachev, open this gate! Mr. Gorbachev, tear down this wall!

—*remarks on East-West relations at the Brandenburg Gate, West Berlin, Germany, June 12, 1987*

In 1961, the Soviet-controlled East Germany built the Berlin Wall. Many world leaders called for the reunification of Germany and the destruction of the wall. In 1989, the Berlin Wall fell, reuniting East and West Berlin and paving the way for German reunification in 1990.

George H. W. Bush

BORN: June 12, 1924
DIED: November 30, 2018
TERM: 1989–1993

I HAVE spoken of a thousand points of light, of all the community organizations that are spread like stars throughout the Nation, doing good. We will work hand in hand, encouraging, sometimes leading, sometimes being led, rewarding. We will work on this in the White House, in the Cabinet agencies. I will go to the people and the programs that are the brighter points of light, and I will ask every member of my government to become involved. The old ideas are new again because they are not old, they are timeless: duty, sacrifice, commitment, and a patriotism that finds its expression in taking part and pitching in.

—*inaugural address, January 20, 1989*

WITH today's signing of the landmark Americans for Disabilities Act, every man, woman, and child with a disability can now pass through once-closed doors into a bright new era of equality, independence, and freedom.

—remarks on signing the Americans with Disabilities Act of 1990, July 26, 1990

THINK about every problem, every challenge, we face. The solution to each starts with education.

—announcement of the America 2000 Education Strategy, April 18, 1991

No nation can fully understand itself or find its place in the world if it does not look with clear eyes at all the glories and disgraces, too, of the past. We in the United States acknowledge such an injustice in our own history: The internment of Americans of Japanese ancestry was a great injustice, and it will never be repeated.

—remarks to World War II veterans and families in Honolulu, Hawai'i, July 12, 1991

Bush's speech referenced the internment of Japanese Americans in prison camps during World War II.

LET all Americans remember that no problem of human making is too great to be overcome by human ingenuity, human energy, and the untiring hope of the human spirit.

—economic address before a joint session of Congress, February 9, 1989

❧ *William J. "Bill" Clinton* ❧

BORN: August 19, 1946
TERM: 1993–2001

I CHALLENGE a new generation of young Americans to a season of service; to act on your idealism by helping troubled children, keeping company with those in need, reconnecting our torn communities. There is so much to be done; enough indeed for millions of others who are still young in spirit to give of themselves in service, too.

—*first inaugural address, January 20, 1993*

THERE is nothing wrong with America that cannot be cured by what is right with America.

—*first inaugural address, January 20, 1993*

I BELIEVE that American citizens who want to serve their country should be able to do so unless their conduct disqualifies them from doing so.

—*press conference, January 29, 1993*

Clinton explained his position regarding the decision to lift the ban excluding homosexual individuals from military service, known as the Don't Ask, Don't Tell policy.

WHILE our nation is enjoying peace and prosperity, too many of our people are still working harder and harder, for less and less. While our businesses are restructuring and growing more productive and competitive, too many of our people still can't be sure of having a job next year or even next month. And far more than our material riches are threatened, things far more precious to us— our children, our families, our values.

—*second State of the Union address, January 24, 1995*

LET us let our own children know that we will stand against the forces of fear. When there is talk of hatred, let us stand up and talk against it. When there is talk of violence, let us stand up and talk against it. In the face of death, let us honor life.

—*remarks at a memorial service for the bombing victims in Oklahoma City, Oklahoma, April 23, 1995*

THE road to tyranny, we must never forget, begins with the destruction of the truth.

—*remarks at the dedication of the Thomas J. Dodd Archives and Research Center in Storrs, Connecticut, October 15, 1995*

MAY those generations whose faces we cannot yet see, whose names we may never know, say of us here that we led our beloved land into a new century with the American dream alive for all her children, with the American promise of a more perfect Union a reality for all her people, with America's bright flame of freedom spreading throughout all the world.

—*second inaugural address, January 20, 1997*

❧ *George W. Bush* ❧

BORN: July 6, 1946
TERM: 2001–2009

CIVILITY is not a tactic or a sentiment. It is the determined choice of trust over cynicism, of community over chaos.

—first inaugural address, January 20, 2001

WHERE there is suffering, there is duty. Americans in need are not strangers, they are citizens, not problems, but priorities. And all of us are diminished when any are hopeless.

—first inaugural address, January 20, 2001

AMERICA was targeted for attack because we're the brightest beacon for freedom and opportunity in the world. And no one will keep that light from shining.

—address to the nation, September 11, 2001

Bush spoke in response to terrorist attacks on the World Trade Center in New York, New York; the Pentagon in Arlington, Virginia; and the plane headed for the US Capitol that was diverted by passengers and crashed in Stonycreek Township, Pennsylvania.

AMERICA is a nation with a mission, and that mission comes from our most basic beliefs. We have no desire to dominate, no ambitions of empire. Our aim is a democratic peace, a peace founded upon the dignity and rights of every man and woman. America acts in this cause with friends and allies at our side, yet we understand our special calling: This great Republic will lead the cause of freedom.

—*third State of the Union address, January 20, 2004*

❧ *Barack Obama* ❧

BORN: August 4, 1961
TERM: 2009–2017

THE time has come to reaffirm our enduring spirit; to choose our better history; to carry forward that precious gift, that noble idea passed on from generation to generation: the God-given promise that all are equal, all are free, and all deserve a chance to pursue their full measure of happiness.

—*first inaugural address, January 20, 2009*

BECAUSE we have tasted the bitter swill of civil war and segregation, and emerged from that dark chapter stronger and more united, we cannot help but believe that the old hatreds shall someday pass; that the lines of tribe shall soon dissolve; that as the world grows smaller, our common humanity shall reveal itself; and that America must play its role in ushering in a new era of peace.

—*first inaugural address, January 20, 2009*

We can acknowledge that oppression will always be with us, and still strive for justice. We can admit the intractability of deprivation, and still strive for dignity. Clear-eyed, we can understand that there will be war, and still strive for peace. We can do that—for that is the story of human progress; that's the hope of all the world; and at this moment of challenge, that must be our work here on Earth.

—*Nobel Prize acceptance speech, December 9, 2009*

The strongest weapon against hateful speech is not repression; it is more speech—the voices of tolerance that rally against bigotry and blasphemy, and lift up the values of understanding and mutual respect.

—*remarks to the United Nations*
General Assembly, September 25, 2012

This is our first task—caring for our children. It's our first job. If we don't get that right, we don't get anything right. That's how, as a society, we will be judged.

—*remarks at the Sandy Hook Interfaith Prayer Vigil*
after the elementary school shooting, December 16, 2012

We are big and vast and diverse; a nation of people with different backgrounds and beliefs, different experiences and stories, but bound by our shared ideal that no matter who you are or what you look like, how you started off, or how and who you love, America is a place where you can write your own destiny.

—*remarks on the Supreme Court decision*
on marriage equality, June 26, 2015

We all have to start with the premise that each of our fellow citizens loves this country just as much as we do; that they value hard work and family just like we do; that their children are just as curious and hopeful and worthy of love as our own.

—farewell address, January 10, 2017

❦ Donald J. Trump ❧

BORN: June 14, 1946
TERM: 2017–2021

What truly matters is not which party controls our government, but whether our government is controlled by the people. January 20th, 2017 will be remembered as the day the people became the rulers of this nation again. The forgotten men and women of our country will be forgotten no longer.

—inaugural address, January 20, 2017

Every child in America should be able to play outside without fear, walk home without danger, and attend a school without being worried about drugs or gangs or violence.

—remarks at the Major Cities Chiefs Association winter conference, February 8, 2017

WE may have our differences, but we do well, in times like these, to remember that everyone who serves in our nation's capital is here because, above all, they love our country. We can all agree that we are blessed to be Americans, that our children deserve to grow up in a nation of safety and peace, and that we are strongest when we are unified and when we work together for the common good.

—*remarks on the shooting of US Representative Steve Scalise of Louisiana in Alexandria, Virginia, June 14, 2017*

OVER the last year, we have made incredible progress and achieved extraordinary success. We have faced challenges we expected, and others we could never have imagined. We have shared in the heights of victory and the pains of hardship. We endured floods and fires and storms. But through it all, we have seen the beauty of America's soul, and the steel in America's spine. Each test has forged new American heroes to remind us who we are, and show us what we can be.

—*first State of the Union address, January 30, 2018*

TODAY we remember those who fell, and we honor all who fought right here in Normandy. They won back this ground for civilization. To more than 170 veterans of the Second World War who join us today: You are among the very greatest Americans who will ever live. You're the pride of our Nation. You are the glory of our Republic. And we thank you from the bottom of our hearts.

—*remarks on the 75th anniversary of the D-Day Allied Forces landing, in Colleville-sur-Mer, France, June 6, 2019*

❧ Joseph R. "Joe" Biden ❧

BORN: November 20, 1942
TERM: 2021–

OUR history has been a constant struggle between the American ideal that we are all created equal and the harsh, ugly reality that racism, nativism, fear, and demonization have long torn us apart. The battle is perennial. Victory is never assured.

—inaugural address, January 20, 2021

To lose a child is like having a piece of your soul ripped away. There's a hollowness in your chest, and you feel like you're being sucked into it and never going to be able to get out. It's suffocating. And it's never quite the same.

—remarks on the school shooting in Uvalde, Texas, May 24, 2022

AMERICA is an idea—the most powerful idea in the history of the world. And it beats in the hearts of the people of this country. It beats in all of our hearts. It unites America. It is the American creed. The idea that America guarantees that everyone be treated with dignity. It gives hate no safe harbor. It installs in everyone the belief that no matter where you start in life, there's nothing you can't achieve. That's who we are. That's what we stand for. That's what we believe.

—address in Philadelphia, Pennsylvania, September 1, 2022